LANDMARK COLLECTOR'S LIBRARY

THE SPIRIT OF

HASLINGDEN

& HELMSHORE

Christopher Aspin & John Simpson

LANDMARK COLLECTOR'S LIBRARY

THE SPIRIT OF
HASLINGDEN
& HELMSHORE

THE 20TH CENTURY IN PHOTOGRAPHS

Christopher Aspin & John Simpson

Landmark Publishing

Published by

Ashbourne Hall, Cokayne Ave
Ashbourne, Derbyshire DE6 1EJ England
Tel: (01335) 347349 Fax: (01335) 347303
e-mail: landmark@clara.net
web site: www.landmarkpublishing.co.uk

ISBN 1 84306 071 X

British Library Cataloguing in Publication Data: a catalogue
record for this book is available from the British Library.

Printed by Bookcraft, Midsomer Norton

Design & reproduction by Mark Titterton

Cover captions:

Front cover: W H Brennards 'Pot Shop', Wilkinson Street

Back cover Top: Market place, 1900

Back cover Middle: Haslingden Corporation marked King George V's
Silver Jubilee in 1935 by illuminating this bus

Back Bottom: The cast of *Boy Blue*, 1956

Title Page: An electric tram approaching the town centre along Blackburn
Road in the 1920s

Contents

Introduction

This is the first Lancashire book in Landmark's admirable series that highlights in pictures the stories of North of England towns and villages during the past century.

In selecting our illustrations of Haslingden and Helmshore, we have kept in mind the essential character of the two places and have taken pains to emphasise the enterprise shown by people in all walks of life to make the district what it is.

Since 1900, changes have been enormous and rapid. Well-known scenes have vanished and totally different ones have replaced them. We have therefore tried to strike a balance between old and new, giving the reader the chance not only to see people of previous generations and some of their achievements, but also to admire the ways in which present-day organisations are keeping the spirit of town and village alive.

The timing of this book has prompted us to give extended coverage to Musbury Church, which celebrates its 150th anniversary this year, and to Haslingden Cricket Club, one of the oldest in Lancashire, which reaches a similar landmark in 2003.

We have borrowed many items from the Helmshore Local History Society's large collection, which has been assembled over the past 50 years, and we have also included photographs borrowed from or taken by many friends and wellwishers. Our sincere thanks are due to all who have contributed material and also to Mike Clarke who enhanced many faded photographs and scanned the rest.

The inclusion of several illustrations that were taken for local newspapers reminds us of the great debt we owe to the Press photographers who, for almost a century, have recorded all aspects of local life. One thinks in particular of Garth Dawson and the late Arthur Constantine, who between them, took thousands of pictures. We are grateful to Mr Dawson and the family of Mr Constantine for permission to include some of their work.

Christopher Aspin and John Simpson

Lizzie Kirby drew this sketch map of Haslingden in 1935, when the town had its own Mayor and Corporation, ran its own buses, schools and library and when Marsden Square (now built over) received regular visits from fun fairs and circuses

Left: St James's Church floodlit during Coronation Week in May, 1937

The town centre during Coronation Week. Note Trinity Baptist Chapel, now demolished

Greenfield Gardens and the war memorial "Courage" on a summer afternoon in 1965

Manchester Road Methodist Church before the adjoining field became the Greenfield Memorial Gardens after World War 1. The church opened for worship in 1857

Whitsuntide, 1928. Members of St James's Church donned period dress to mark the centenary of the rebuilding of the tower

Familiar products, including Colman's Mustard, Stork Margarine and Crawford's biscuits, can be picked out on the horse-drawn cart that joined the May Day parade in 1910. The picture was taken in Marsden Square. Mr J H Pilling is on the right and Norman Hamer on the left

No. 12 Higher Deardengate in the early 1900s, when it was the house and workshop of John Richard Hargreaves, plumber and glazier. The business was founded by his grandfather, who bought the property in 1859. It was originally a warehouse and stable belonging to the Rawsthorne family

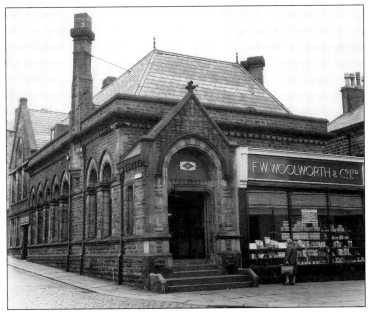

F W Woolworth's store in Higher Deardengate occupied a building that began life in the 1870s as a branch of the Manchester and Liverpool District Bank. When the premises were completed, Parsonage Lane was renamed Bank Street. The store, which opened in 1954 and closed in 1970, was one of the smallest in the Woolworth chain. The picture was taken in 1965

Church processions always stopped in the Market Place for hymn singing. *Above:* Trinity Baptists, many of the men wearing straw hats, in the early 1920s. *Below:* Primitive Methodists at a slightly earlier date

St James's Whit processions. *Above:* Lower Deardengate in 1948 and *below*, at the junction of Blackburn Road and John Street in 1966

The last tram to Accrington and the first bus to Bacup. Haslingden centre on May 1, 1930, when the new service took over from the old. Richard Bowker, vice chairman of the Transport Committee, holds the starting handle of the bus

Large crowds watched the funeral in 1911 of John Lawrence Whittaker, solicitor, Liberal and nonconformist. Here the procession makes its way up Pleasant Street to Ebenezer Baptist Church in Bury Road

The windows of Robert Bamford's shop at 6 and 8 Prinny Hill have just been decorated with advertising slogans by the artist in the straw hat. The date is 1913. Mr Bamford is chatting to the people on the right of the picture; his wife Amelia is in the shop door

William Henry Brennard and his wife Mary ran their glass and china warehouse, better known as The Pot Shop, at 5, Wilkinson Street from 1888 until 1928. Mrs Brennand, who died in 1933, aged 88, was one of the 15 children of John Cordingley, court bailiff and grandfather of J S Cordingley, founder of the motor business

Left: A 1960s window display in the Haslingden Electricity Showroom, Higher Deardengate

Below: Lower Deardengate in 1965. The bank on the right has served townspeople since 1914. It was opened by the Manchester and County Bank, later absorbed by the District. NatWest followed

Right: The Public Baths soon after their opening in 1936 and some 28 years after they were first proposed. The wall and railings have since been removed

Left: Haslingden firemen practise rescue techniques at the Drill Hall, where they were based in 1898. Soon afterwards the brigade moved to a permanent fire station at the Public Hall in Regent Street

Below: Haslingden Fire Brigade's annual inspection in 1935. The Fire Station was then at the Public Hall in Regent Street. The Mayor is Councillor Fred Brandwood. Oates Maden, the Chief Fire Officer, is on the right

Charles Lane and Hutch Bank in the early 1900s. Note the houses on the steep hillside

Heavy snow blocks Helmshore Road in 1910. The photograph was taken at a point near the present entrance to Rawsthorne Avenue

How things looked in 1900. Workpeople's houses and cotton mills stand between the railway station in the foreground and the parish church, top right. Much of the development followed the arrival of the East Lancashire Railway in 1848

Haslingden, looking west, in 1900. The parish church is on the right and Hargreaves Street Mill on the left. Between them was Top of the Town, the oldest part of Haslingden

Market Place in about 1900. Next to the Swan Hotel is a branch of Altham's, the tea and travel firm

Council workmen removing the Big Lamp from the Market Place on 11 December, 1962. It had become a hazard to traffic. Mr Donald Heyworth bought the lamp and re-erected it in the garden of his home, Rothdene, in Helmshore Road

The steps of the Police Station in George Street (formerly the Town Hall) were used on March 15, 1905, for an auction of goods belonging to nonconformists who refused to pay an education rate. The 1902 Education Act integrated denominational schools into the state system and provided for their support from the rates. Nonconformists, who objected to supporting Anglicans, set up a National Passive Resistance Committee and a Citizens' League, opposed the Act in Haslingden. Police distrained goods of people who refused to pay the rate. By 1905, the number of passive resisters in the town had fallen to seven

Working women in clogs and shawls left the mills at Rising Bridge to watch the funeral at Stonefold Church in 1915

King Street Methodist Church and Sunday School, of which only the small graveyard survives. The chapel opened in 1798 and was used until the larger church in Manchester Road was completed in 1857. Some eleven years later, King Street re-opened because the new building could not meet the demand for pews

Arthur Kirby's sketch of Bury Road as it looked in the 1920s. Arthur was born in the family grocery and corn shop on the right of the picture. He attended the Grammar School (now gone) and married in Ebenezer Baptist Church, which has been much altered

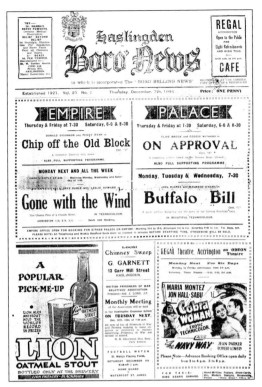

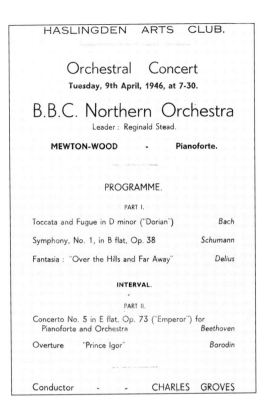

Above left: The front page of the *Haslingden Boro' News* for December 7, 1944. The newspaper began in 1921 as the *Boro' Selling News*, a free sheet that supported the Labour movement, but in 1945 it was taken over by a group of local businessmen. The *Rochdale Observer* bought the title in 1974 and ran the paper until December 18, 1984. *Above right:* At the invitation of Haslingden Arts Club, the BBC Northern Orchestra broadcast several times from the Public Hall. Here is the programme for a concert on 9 April, 1946

Left: The Blackburn Road area of Haslingden taken by Garth Dawson from the tower of St James's Church during the July holidays in 1953. Many of the buildings have gone, among them Commercial Mill (lower left) and Springside cottages (lower right). The railway still had thirteen years of life before it fell to Dr Beeching's axe and provided a foundation for the by-pass. In the fields (top left) is Haslingden Steam Laundry

Haslingden railway station in 1960, six years before its demolition with the closure of the line between Accrington and Stubbins. The picture was taken from the North Hag, which was removed to make way for the Haslingden by-pass. The chimneys are (from the left): Britannia Mill, Carr Mill and Albert Mill

Above: The brick core (eight layers) of Haslingden railway tunnel was exposed during the summer of 1980 when workmen building the Haslingden by-pass removed 500,000 tons of rock and sand that formed the North Hag adjoining the station

Left: Wesley Methodist Chapel was built near the junction of Blackburn Road and Hudhey Road in 1884. It closed in 1971 and was then used by Sirdar Fabrics as a textile printworks. The building was demolished in 1982

A garden party at Carterplace Hall in the early 1900s. The owner in the early part of the century was the cotton manufacturer Tom Worsley who died in 1923, leaving among other possessions, a celebrated collection of orchids

Rising Bridge seen from the air in 1965. The railway still had a year's life before it closed and one can see a diesel train approaching the road bridge near the school. From this height it was possible to read "Holland's Pies" on the chimney of the Baxenden factory

Above: The George and Dragon, Stonefold, shortly before its closure in 1959. The inn, which stood on the King's Highway linking Haslingden and Huncoat, was kept by members of the Parkinson family in the late 18th and early 19th centuries

Left: The Baxenden premises of Walter Holland & Son began life as a cotton factory, providing a tall chimney that was ideal, until its demolition on September 9, 1980, for promoting the famous pies. The photograph was taken in the 1960s

Left: Haslingden grew rapidly during the 19th and early 20th centuries as the cotton trade expanded. More than 20 mills, including Stonefold (seen here in the 1920s) spun thread and wove cloth

Albert Buildings at the bottom of Pleasant Street in 1903. Above the shops, young men misspent their youth playing billiards in the Albert Hall. James Edward Hoyle, painter and decorator, owned the property, which included Heywood's Market, also known as a "fancy repository". The third shop belonged to John Rishton, music and musical instrument dealer, who was a violinist with Haslingden Orchestral Society from its formation. J E Hoyle bought the old Baptist Chapel and adjoining property in Pleasant Street in the 1880s and erected Albert Buildings on the site

Hindle Street Mission, built in 1889 by Canon Champneys, did much to help the poor in the old part of the town. This photograph, taken in 1965, also shows the Grammar School on the far side of Bury Road

Haslingden Municipal Offices in Bury Road was originally West View, the home of the Woodcock family. It was built in the 1850s and remained one of the few brick houses in the town for almost a century. Haslingden Council bought the building in 1894 and added the council chamber at the rear. It was demolished in 1999

Members and chief officers of Haslingden Borough Council in November, 1983, shortly before its amalgamation with Bacup and Rawtenstall to form the Rossendale authority. The Mayor, Alderman Donald Butterworth, is flanked by the Town Clerk, Robert Bruce McMillan, and the Deputy Mayor, Coun. Tom Fisher

Deardengate House (now demolished) was the birthplace of the composer Alan Rawsthorne. He is seen here with his parents and sister in about 1908. Members of the Rawsthorne family lived in the house for more than 100 years. They were woolstaplers, putting out warp and weft to weavers; and they used the top storey, which was one long room, as a warehouse. Haslingden Borough Council bought the house in 1909 so that part of it could be taken down to enable Helmshore Road to be widened. The rest survived until the early 1960s

Manchester Road Wesleyan Day School, demolished in 1981 to make way for the Health Centre, is remembered as the building in which a group of Haslingden students took the world's first intelligence test. It was the idea of Mr (later Sir) William Mather, the MP for Rossendale and a Manchester industrialist. He was worried by German competition and felt that the better use of intelligence by British workpeople would help to counter the threat. He therefore proposed an intelligence test and offered a prize of £5 for the student who did best. Mr H Holman, a forward-looking Inspector of Schools, set the questions and marked the papers following the test on December 13, 1901. John Thomas Heap, a young weaver in a local cotton mill, won the prize. One of the questions: "Which would you rather have — a ton of sovereigns or two tons of half sovereigns?"

Major David Halstead playing games with children during a garden party at his home Highfield, in the early 1900s. His son-in-law Arthur Watson, later Mayor of Haslingden, looks on. Highfield has been replaced by a nursing home

Todd Hall, close to the present industrial estate at Carrs, was unusual for an 18th century building in having four storeys. Some parts were much older

Flaxmoss Garage (now replaced by Jubilee Garage) in 1930. It was run by the Moorhouse family. Pictured are Will Moorhouse (left), Will Moorhouse Jnr, and George Haywood

Right: Tuesday, January 12, 1982, saw the demolition of Size House Mill chimney by the celebrity steeplejack Fred Dibnah. The business had closed four years earlier. Flats known as Size House Village now occupy the site between Manchester Road and Back Lane

The Road End district of Haslingden in the late 1940s. Syke and Sykeside Mills were then busily making cotton goods in the boom that followed World War II. Sykeside Mill was built

in 1836 by James Stott and Thomas Smith, woollen manufacturers, who came from Edenfield. The owners were devout Methodists and built a mission room at the bottom of Mill Street.

John Warburton Ltd. acquired the mill in 1907 and changed to cotton. R S Wills, who bought the business from Highams in 1970, ceased production in 1999. Fire badly damaged the mill on Good Friday, April 13, 2001, as one can see from the photograph taken by the Vicar of Musbury, the Rev Norman Price. The chimney was reduced to half its height in April 2002 and the whole site was closed soon afterwards to make way for a garden centre

Touch and Take, handloom weavers' cottages built in the late 18th century, stood off Manchester Road between Road End and the Woolpack. The name is said to derive from a frequent saying of an old lady who kept a shop in one of the houses: "If you touch anything, you must take it"

Building the Haslingden By-pass. The view from Hutch Bank in the spring of 1981

Left: The Haslingden Auction Mart Company operated in a range of buildings at Bentgate from 1910 until its closure to make way for housing, in 2000. Sheep and cattle sales attracted farmers from a wide area

Right: Farmers' vehicles fill the car park in Private Lane in 1999, shortly before the auction mart closed

A photograph taken during the auction mart's Christmas Show in 1950. Left to right: John Procter (director), Joseph Balshaw (auctioneer), William Bolton (judge), Maurice McCann (secretary), James Edward Barlow (chairman), Charles Simpson (director), Jacob Warburton (director), C Lawson (judge), Norman Duxbury (auctioneer and director)

Bidding for cattle during the 1960s

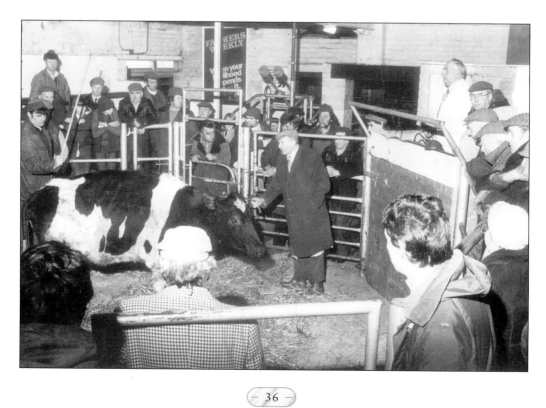

For much of the 19th and 20th centuries, cotton and woollen mills provided work for most Haslingden and Helmshore people. The clatter of Lancashire looms in large weaving sheds is heard no more. The Grane Manufacturing Company in Back Lane had 1,000 looms, two of which are shown in a photograph taken during the Coronation celebrations in 1953

Members of Haslingden Lawn Tennis Club relaxing after a match in 1947. The clubhouse and courts adjoined the Cricket Club and Private Lane and tennis was played until the late 1950s. From the left: Jean Rideough, Vera Cartin, Marie Rideough, Norma Shepherd-Walsh and Pat Weir

Two pictures from the 1950s remind us that Haslingden had many organisations that have ceased to exist and that they usually invited civic leaders to their functions. *Left:* The Mayor and Mayoress, Coun. and Mrs J W Holgate at a Young Farmers' social evening in 1954; and *below*, Coun and Mrs Joe Everett, guests of honour at Haslingden Liberal Association's annual ball in 1956

Left: Broadway and Flaxmoss seen from the air in 1961. Rydal Road was taking shape in the foreground, but the estate of prefabricated houses beside Lancaster Avenue (left) was nearing the end of its life. On the right of the picture is the group of houses known as The Fields

Personalities

Above: Major's Sunday, 1931. Standing outside the Municipal Offices in Bury Road are (left to right): Major David Halstead, local historian and former MP for Rossendale; Alderman Jerry Lord; the Mayor, Councillor, A S Watson; the Town Clerk; Mr T Oldroyd and the Mayor's chaplain, the Rev T W Hodson, vicar of St James's

"He helped them to look at the stars", the inscription on his gravestone in Musbury churchyard, sums up the remarkable career of John Henry Hindle (1869-1942), the factory lad, who became a leading builder of large reflecting telescopes.

Mr Hindle was born at Edenfield; and though he began work as a half-timer when he was twelve and a half, he spent his spare moments in an iron foundry and developed an interest in precision engineering, in particular the development of electrical equipment, for which he held a number of patents. In 1918, he took over the Union Engineering Works in Haslingden, where he designed and built machinery for the cotton trade. Mr Hindle made his first telescope mirror in 1910, and 25 years later was a world authority on the subject. Among the many large reflecting telescopes he built was his own 25-inch Newtonian reflector pictured here. The Hindle Test for telescope mirrors is still used

Arthur John Chappell, a journalist who wrote under the pen-name of "Briar", is seen here compiling a report on a cricket match at Bentgate. Mr Chappell, a native of Glossop, came to Haslingden in 1892. He worked as a free-lance reporter and on the *Haslingden Gazette* until 1925, when he became district reporter for the *Haslingden Observer*. Mr Chappell died in 1956, aged 88

Tom Worsley (1884-1923), a prominent figure in the cotton trade – the family firm, N Worsley Ltd, was the largest in the hard waste sector – generously supported organisations and good causes throughout his short life. As well as being a Town Councillor, he was president of Haslingden Cricket Club, the Subscription Bowling Club and the Borough Band. Mr Worsley lived at Carterplace Hall, where he indulged his passion for orchids.

The 1923 sale catalogue of the "Carterplace Collection" includes a cypripedium named after Mr Worsley. "Cypripediums", says the introduction to the catalogue, "were the late owner's especial favourites, and every care was bestowed, and no expense spared in keeping the collection up-to-date and in first-class condition as regards culture. The splendid displays of cypripedium flowers at Carterplace have been a feature of these gardens for several years; and we venture to say it will be difficult to find better, or more strongly grown plants of cypripediums anywhere"

56 **TOM WORSLEY.** (Actæus Langleyense x Helen II). F.C.C.M.O.S. 1916. A very beautiful and refined Cypm. The flower is of good size, and carried well, and of thick texture ; dorsal sepal clear white, with sparse violet rose spottings, petals and pouch a lovely shade of soft rich yellow. Though not a very large flower, this is a most charming and quite distinct Cypm, and if only on account of its daintiness and refinement, is worth a place in the best Collection. **Splendid plant.** 5 very fine large growths **7 7 0**

Haslingden Grammar School Sports Day in 1932. The playing field between Broadway and Greens Lane is now occupied by the High School. The school was divided into houses, Holcombe, Grane, Cribden and Musbury. The Mayor, Ald A S Watson presented the prizes. On his right is the headmaster, Mr Arnold Weston. Standing (extreme left) is Mr E W J Moore, science master and amateur geologist, after whom a fossil is named and (second right) Dr G H Tuping, history master and author of *The Economic History of Rossendale*

Sir Horace Smirk, for many years a leading figure in the New Zealand medical establishment and a world authority on blood pressure, was born at Baxenden in 1902, the son of Thomas Smirk, the first headmaster of Haslingden Grammar School. At the time of his retirement in 1968, Sir Horace was Research Professor and Director at Wellcome Medical Research Institute at the University of Otago Medical School. He was made a KBE in 1958

To the Electors of SYKE WARD

11 Colldale Terrace,
28th March, 1947.

Dear Ladies and Gentlemen,

You will have seen in the local papers that I am contesting Syke Ward as a Labour representative.

I admit my youth, but feel as many of you will know, that my earlier political activities qualify me for this step. Also, the vigour and vision of youth linked with the wisdom and experience of our older municipal representatives should produce the happy medium.

I served during the last war in the Navy in the Far East and know thoroughly the thoughts and needs of the returned ex-serviceman, but it is as a man of peace with constructive and not destructive ideas that I want to appeal to you. I am a man believing in the building up of the resources of this country for the use of all and everyone of us; a country of full employment, social security, equality of education, of opportunity, run and controlled by its people, yet a country where human values are honoured.

I realise the urgency of housing and similar schemes— I myself, as a married ex-serviceman unable to get a house, appreciate the position as well as anyone, and I will do all in my power to remedy it. I believe in the building up of towns like Haslingden into larger centres of population able to give their citizens full services; and not in the enlargement of already large centres and the decrease of towns like ours. New light industries are needed here.

I believe in a form of strong world government to prevent another war—a war which would end in the suicide of man in atomic warfare. Don't trust the Tories and Imperialists we don't want a '14 or '39 again.

I promise you solid sincere service ; no vain promises I do not intend to keep. I shall not be able to see you all before the election, so I take this opportunity of appealing for your support on April 9th — a vote for progress and the future.

Yours sincerely,

RHODES BOYSON.

HASLINGDEN
Municipal Bye-Elections

April 9th, 1947.

SYKE WARD

LET LABOUR BUILD
A More Prosperous Haslingden

RHODES BOYSON

Sir Rhodes Boyson, the Conservative MP for Brent North from 1974 to 1997 and a member of Mrs Thatcher's government, was born in Hoyle Street, Rising Bridge, in 1927. He attended Stonefold School and Haslingden Grammar School. Sir Rhodes began his political career in the Labour Party and in 1947 unsuccessfully fought Syke Ward, securing 1,043 votes. His Conservative opponent, George Hargreaves Tomlinson, won the by-election with 1,523

Haslingden Council's highest honour — the Freedom of the Borough — was bestowed on three citizens in 1947. At a special meeting of the Town Council, the Mayor, Coun James Moran, presented scrolls and caskets to Alderman Jeremiah Lord (left), Nurse Annie Mary Knowles and Alderman Arthur Watson. The two aldermen were former Mayors and Nurse Knowles had been a district nurse for more than 30 years

The composer Alan Rawsthorne (1905-1971) was born at Deardengate House (demolished) and later lived at Sykeside House, now a restaurant and hotel, where a blue plaque marks the link. Because of parental opposition to a musical career, Rawsthorne reluctantly studied dentistry and architecture before going to the Royal Manchester College of Music at the age of 20. He won many admirers with his *Symphonic Variations*, first performed at a concert of the International Society for Contemporary Music in Warsaw in 1939. Rawsthorne composed three symphonies, concertos, much chamber music, *Practical Cats* for speaker and orchestra (poems by T S Eliot) and scores for several films, including *The Cruel Sea*. Much of his work has been recorded

Haslingden Grammar School's teaching staff in 1954. The headmaster, Mr Arnold Weston, is seated, fourth from the right. On his right is Mr J W Lewis, deputy head and physics master

For more than fory years, The Jack Taylor Band played for dances and shows, including the pantomimes staged by St Mary's Church. From the left: Roy Mason, Jack Taylor, Arthur Frost (pianist) and Eddie Holden

Left: Jack Cordingley with his Formula 1 JBW Maserati after winning the Maidstone and Mid-Kent International Event at Silverstone in 1964. Jack spent his working life as a motor dealer in the family showrooms at the junction of Warner Street and Lower Deardengate

Below left: Professor Tom Constantine, an old boy of Haslingden Grammar School, was Acting Vice Chancellor of Salford University for six years until his death in 1981. Tom, son of Arthur and Jane Alice Constantine, became the university's second professor of civil engineering in 1967 and chairman of the department two years later. A purpose-built complex at the university was named Constantine Court as a memorial to a man who led by example and who built up one of the largest civil engineering departments in the United Kingdom

Above: Jim Ramsbottom (stage name Hans Lindhuber) won a talent competition at Haslingden Public Hall in 1961 and went on to become a professional entertainer. His act included whistling, yodelling, singing, playing the ukulele and novel effects with spoons and bones. For more than 20 years, Jim performed in theatres, clubs, cabaret and on TV. He specialised in family entertainment and Tyrolen shows, one of which ran for twelve successive seasons at St Annes

Russian-born Natasha Grishin, who spent her teenage years in Haslingden, enjoyed a successful career as a dancer in the United States. Her father, the late Professor Peter Grishin, a distinguished textile scientist, worked for TMM (Research) in Helmshore before settling in America. Natasha attended Haslingden Grammar School and won many prizes for ballet as a pupil of Miss Beatrice Shipstone. Natasha was a member of the *corps-de-ballet* at the New York Metropolitan Opera before going on to a career in show business. She is at the centre of this group of dancers that delighted audiences in the 1960s production of the Broadway musical *How to Succeed in Business Without Really Trying*

Gerald Birtwell rode for Nelson in the British National League during the late 1960s after training at the Belle Vue club in Manchester. His motor-cycle was a 500cc JAP

Tony Greenwood, MP for Rossendale and Housing Minster in the Labour Government, cuts a tape to open the Central Square flats in September, 1967

Father (later Canon) Herbert Rigby joins in a game of skittles with children from St Mary's Church at an event to mark his retirement in 1984

In 1976, Arthur Hambley, a retired cabinetmaker, built a spinning machine based on drawings made by Leonardo da Vinci in the 15th century. It was made for Helmshore Local History Society at his home in Park Avenue. Arthur proves to friends and neighbours that Leonardo could have started the Industrial Revolution more than 400 years before it actually began. Jack Taylor is on the left

Sir David Trippier visiting Holland's during his time as Rossendale's MP (1979 to 1992). With him is supervisor Fred Pickup. Sir David, who lives in Helmshore, was High Sheriff for Lancashire 1997-98

At a time of life, when most people put their feet up, Bill Grimshaw, of Holden Bank Farm, learned to fly a helicopter and then took up motor racing. In both 2001 and 2002, he came second in the British Formula Junior Class championship. Here he is at Silverstone in his Gemini car, which has a top speed of 130 mph. *Below:* Bill with his Robinson R22 helicopter on the landing strip behind his home

Left: Alan McPartland, "The Valley Tailor", opened his Manchester Road shop in 1980. Now he is one of the last bespoke tailors in Lancashire

Below: Kevin Grogan keeps alive the ancient craft of dry-stone walling. Here he is working at Fish Tenement Barn, off Grane Road

Members of the Vounteer League parade at Kirkhill on a frosty day in February, 1915

Haslingden remembers Edith Cavell, the English Nurse executed in Belgium by the Germans during the First World War after being accused of spying for the Allies. Here the procession makes its way up Church Street before a service at St James's

The Government rewarded Haslingden for its contribution to World War I by donating a tank, which was displayed close to the clock tower in Victoria Park. It was sold for scrap in 1927

NCOs of the Haslingden Home Guard in 1941. Most had served in World War I

Haslingden High Street students Stacey Keyes and Vickie Macdonald examine a relic of World War II that has survived close to the school playing field in Greens Lane. The railway sleeper was one of several hundred driven into the ground between Broadway and Greens Lane to deter enemy aircraft from landing

This concrete pillbox on the hillside above Holcombe Road is one of the few survivors from the hundreds built during the early part of World War II as Britain prepared for a German invasion

Learning how to cope with incendiary bombs. This group of volunteers went into action at Prinny Hill. The man on the ground is Harry Haworth, who had a confectioner's shop in Ratcliffe Street

The Holden Vale Manufacturing Company helped the RAF to win the Battle of Britain in 1940 by producing the propellant for incendiary bullets fired from Hurricanes and Spitfires. The work remained a secret for more than fifty years, and most of the workers were unaware of the significance of their efforts. But it is now known that the bullets played a decisive part in repulsing the German assault. The Luftwaffe lacked this weapon, which destroyed many of their planes.

The company was set up in 1938 following a deal between the Bleachers' Association and the Hercules Powder Co. Inc., of the United States. It produced cellulose products from chemical cotton that helped not only our fighter pilots, but also bomber crews by improving tyre safety. Towards the end of the war, the company also developed a filler for small rockets that enabled planes to take off with heavy bomb loads.

Radar, our means of detecting enemy aircraft, improved greatly when the Holden Wood boffins, headed by Colin Colman, developed an improved condenser tissue.

After the war, cellulose made at Holden Wood found many peaceful uses: x-ray film, plastic for toys, toothbrush handles, drawing and writing paper and thickening agents for sauces, cosmetics and pharmaceuticals.

The old works has been replaced by an hotel, conference centre, health club and restaurant

The Girls' Training Corps and supporters in 1942. Drill, first-aid and the Morse Code were among the subjects taught to prepare the teenagers for service with the Armed Forces. The Mayoress, Mrs Watson, is second from the right on the front row

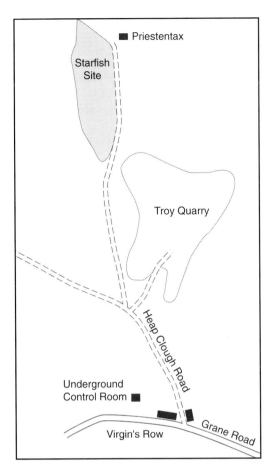

Left: The RAF built a decoy railway marshalling yard, known officially as a Starfish site, at Heap Clough in 1941. Its purpose was to protect Blackburn and the surrounding industrial areas by deceiving enemy bombers. The control room was behind Virgin's Row, from which cables ran to mock rail wagons in a field below Priestentax. These could be set on fire and it was hoped that a second wave of enemy aircraft would attack the site, thinking the first bombers had succeeded in finding an important taget. The site was never activated

Below: Airmen on the Heap Clough Starfish site in 1940. The tree on the right is at Priestentax, where the men converted an old pigsty into a rest room. Jack Standen (top left), Bill Bedford (extreme left, middle row) and Alan Brown (second from right, middle row) married Haslingden girls. The unit took over part of the former Grane Vicarage as an office

The Air Training Corps marching through the Market Place during Wings for Victory Week in 1943

A World War II flag united Haslingden with the Seychelles, Mauritius and Rodrigues. Islanders who served in Egypt under Major Ervin Russell, of Haslingden, wished to fly their own flag over unit headquarters and, having included the names of their countries, added the home town of their commanding officer. Major Russell returned to Haslingden with the flag in 1945; and 52 years later, his son Derek presented it to the Military Museum in Port Louis, Mauritius. The picture shows Derek and his son Andrew with the flag shortly before its return.

When the Eighth Army invaded Italy, Major Russell was one of the first British soldiers to enter Rome, where he found the flag of one of Mussolini's crack regiments flying over the building he made his HQ.

More than 30 years later, Derek became friendly with a group of former Italian soldiers who were guests at an Eighth Army reunion. They invited him to visit them, and in their old regimental building Derek saw a picture of the flag his father captured:

"My new friends would not believe me when I told them I had the real thing, but when I went again I presented it to them. Now they use it as an altar cloth in their chapel"

Workers at J H Birtwistle's cotton mill in Grane Road amused townspeople and collected money with their village wedding procession during Wings for Victory Week

Ladies' Day during Wings for Victory Week. The indicator board on spare land now occupied by the Fire Station shows that the target of £100,000 had almost been reached. This was enough to buy two Lancaster bombers and four Spitfire fighters. By the end of the week, the appeal had raised £151,170, equal to £10 for each person living in the town

The ATC on parade during Wings for Victory Week

In 1944, Flash Mill beat more than 300 mills and workshops in the textile trade to win a competition for War Savings. The mill employed 100 operatives, each of whom saved on average 13s (65p) a week. The picture shows the workforce with a trophy presented by Lord Derby

Left: A fund-raising procession in Bury Road during Salute the Soldier Week in 1944. The penny-farthing bicycle, owned and ridden by George Berry, and the boneshaker had taken part in the Coronation procession in 1937, hence the date on the sign

Right: The ATC marching up Manchester Road, Haslingden, in 1945

Left: King George VI and Queen Elizabeth visited Haslingden on March 8, 1945. Here the Mayor, Alderman A S Watson, introduces the King to Alderman Jerry Lord. Alderman William Boyson and Mrs Boyson are also in the picture

Haslingden Cricket Club

Haslingden Cricket Club was formed in 1853 and has played throughout its history on the Bentgate ground. The club won the Lancashire League Championship in 1900, 1920, 1953, 1983, 1985, 1987, 1988, 1989, 1991, 1993 and 1997. It also won the Worsely Cup in 1921, 1977, 1992, 1993 and 1997

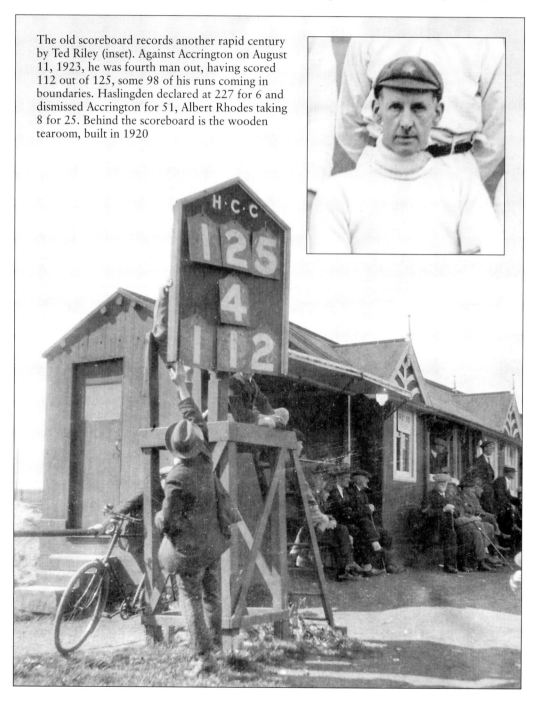

The old scoreboard records another rapid century by Ted Riley (inset). Against Accrington on August 11, 1923, he was fourth man out, having scored 112 out of 125, some 98 of his runs coming in boundaries. Haslingden declared at 227 for 6 and dismissed Accrington for 51, Albert Rhodes taking 8 for 25. Behind the scoreboard is the wooden tearoom, built in 1920

George Headley, the West Indian Test Cricketer, was Haslingden's professional from 1934 to 1938. In 1937, he scored 1,360 runs, including five centuries, for an average of 97.15. When Headley signed for the club, membership doubled to 893; and some 24,102 people paid to see games at Bentgate in 1934

Haslingden 1ˢᵗ XI, Lancashire League champions in 1953. Standing: Leonard Pilkington, Norman Greenwell, Jack Cronkshaw, Gordon Pilkington, Raymond Scott, John Winter, David Hardman. Seated: Albert Riley, Billy Aldred, J W H Gastall (Captain), Vinoo Mankad (professional), John Ingham. The picture was taken in front of the old tearoom

After receiving the cup, the team toured Haslingden in an open-topped coach

John Ingham, J W H Gastall and Vinco Mankad with the championship trophy

FINAL AVERAGES, 1953.

BOWLING.

	Overs	Runs	W.	Aver.
J. Ingham (Haslingden)	208.3	705	71	9.92
Mankad (Haslingden)	347.6	850	85	10.00
McCool (East Lancs.)	260	948	93	10.19
S. Hall (Bacup)	207.7	560	51	10.98
Umrigar (Church)	317.6	814	68	11.97
Pepper (Burnley)	329.1	1098	88	12.47
Denison (Todmorden)	268.2	835	66	12.65
T. E. Dickinson (E. Lancs.)	73	178	14	12.71
A. Bourke (Church)	166.9	497	38	13.07
T. Lowe (Church)	200.3	627	47	13.36
Walker (Rawtenstall)	256.5	795	59	13.47
Walcott (Enfield)	260	707	52	13.59

John Ingham topped the league bowling averages with 71 wickets and Mankad, the Indian Test player, was second with 85 wickets. Mankad was also third in the batting averages (856 runs at 50.35) and Ingham 11th with 423 runs at 30.00

Left: Clive Lloyd, Haslingden's professional in 1967 and '68, going out to bat from the old pavilion with John Winter in the match against Nelson on September 1, 1968. Clive scored 119 not out and completed 1,000 runs, his total for the season being 1,226 (61.60). Clive went on to play for Lancashire and captain the West Indies. John played 490 games for the 1st XI between 1947 and 1976

Below: John Entwistle (right), president of the club, receives a picture of the new pavilion, opened in 1967, which is named after him. The presentation was arranged by the players as a thank you to Mr Entwistle for his work and financial help with the much needed development. Also pictured are John Ingham, William Burton (committee) and Bill Grimshaw

Left: Michael Ingham and his father John played together in the Haslingden 1st XI in 1974, when this picture was taken, Michael, who was 17, played seven innings, including an unbeaten 50 at Church. His batting average of 54 was the best in the league that season

The Haslingden players celebrate their 1977 Worsley Cup success in the dressing room. Wicket-keeper Tony White pours the champagne into the trophy, which is held by the captain Tony Holden; Bill Grimshaw; and the professional, Peter Swart

Bryan Knowles, seen here in the nets at Bentgate, was the third Lancashire League amateur to top 1,000 runs in a single season. He achieved the feat in 1981 when he also headed the league averages. In a career that began in 1966 and ended in 1992, Bryan played 544 league innings and made a total of 13,091 runs. He scored 500 runs in a season 16 times. Bryan captained the League Cricket Conference XI against India, Sri Lanka and Australia

Matthew Brown
Lancashire Cricket League.

BATTING AVERAGES 1981

	Inns.	NO	Runs	Average
B. Knowles (Haslingden)	25	3	1050	47.73
Lal (Enfield)	24	5	895	47.10
G. Beech (Accrington)	25	5	938	46.90
Khan (Todmorden)	22	3	871	45.84
Dev. (Nelson)	21	1	880	44.00
McArdle (Church)	22	3	827	43.52
Stead (Accrington)	25	6	821	43.21
O'Neill (East Lancs.)	21	2	774	40.74
Amarnath (Lowerhouse)	23	3	766	38.30
P. G. Wood (Rawtenstall)	22	4	687	38.16
I. Clarkson (Nelson)	25	2	823	35.78

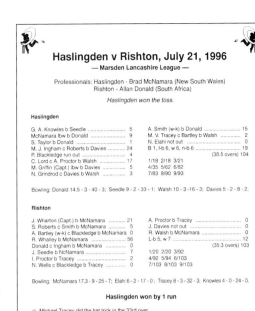

Haslingden v Rishton, July 21, 1996
— Marsden Lancashire League —

Professionals: Haslingden - Brad McNamara (New South Wales)
Rishton - Allan Donald (South Africa)

Haslingden won the toss.

Haslingden

G. A. Knowles b Seedle	5	A. Smith (w-k) b Donald		15
McNamara lbw b Donald	9	M. V. Tracey c Bartley b Walsh		2
S. Taylor b Donald	1	N. Elahi not out		0
M. J. Ingham c Roberts b Davies	24	B 1, l-b 6, w 6, n-b 6		19
P. Blackledge run out	4		(38.5 overs)	104
C. Lord c A. Proctor b Walsh	17			
M. Griffin (Capt.) lbw b Davies	5	1/18 2/18 3/21		
N. Grindrod c Davies b Walsh	3	4/35 5/62 6/82		
		7/83 8/90 9/93		

Bowling: Donald 14.5 - 3 - 40 - 3; Seedle 9 - 2 - 33 - 1; Walsh 10 - 3 -16 - 3; Davies 5 - 2 - 8 - 2.

Rishton

J. Wharton (Capt.) b McNamara	21	A. Proctor b Tracey		0
S. Roberts c Smith b McNamara	5	J. Davies not out		0
A. Bartley (w-k) c Blackledge b McNamara	0	R. Walsh b McNamara		0
R. Whalley b McNamara	56	L-b 5, w 7		12
Donald c Ingham b McNamara	0		(35.3 overs)	103
J. Seedle b McNamara	7	1/20 2/20 3/92		
I. Proctor b Tracey	2	4/92 5/94 6/103		
N. Wells c Blackledge b Tracey	0	7/103 8/103 9/103		

Bowling: McNamara 17.3 - 9 - 25 - 7; Elahi 6 - 2 - 17 - 0; Tracey 8 - 3 - 32 - 3; Knowles 4 - 0 - 24 - 0.

Haslingden won by 1 run

 Michael Tracey did the hat trick in the 33rd over.

 When Rishton lost their third wicket, they needed 13 runs to win with 20 overs remaining. When their fifth wicket fell, they needed 11 runs with 18 overs remaining. When the sixth wicket fell, they needed 2 runs with 13 overs remaining.

 The last five wickets fell for no runs, and the last eight wickets for 11 runs.

 No runs were scored during the final 21 minutes of the game, during which 23 balls were bowled.

Above left: A record partnership. Against Church at Bentgate in 1985, Ian Austin (left) scored 149 not out and John Entwistle 106 not out. They shared an unbroken third-wicket partnership of 268, the highest for any club since the league was formed in 1892. Ian went on to play for Lancashire and England; and in 2001 returned to Haslingden as professional

Above right: The glorious uncertainty of cricket. Haslingden v Rishton 1996

Twenty two-year-old Graham Knowles, elder son of Bryan, made 183 not out for Haslingden at Rawtenstall in 1996, a record by an amateur in limited-overs cricket. He hit seven sixes and 18 fours and shared 150 stands with Michael Ingham and professional Brad McNamara. Haslingden made 301 for 1

Miss Clara Worsley, of Carterplace Hall, was Rose Queen in 1911 when Haslingden
celebrated the Coronation of King George V

The children's corner, Victoria Park, in 1905

May Day in Commerce Street, Carrs, in the 1920s. The district is now an industrial estate

A children's room opened in the Public Library in 1931. Here are pupils from the elementary schools in the town with the Mayor, Alderman A S Watson; Alderman T F Haworth, Chairman of the Library Committee; and Miss L Hurd, the Borough Librarian

In November, 1932, Haslingden Grammar School pupils, all aged under 15, gave an operetta *Snow White and the Seven Dwarfs* and a play *The Prince who was a Piper*. Neil McTaggart (left) produced the operetta

Above: Flower power. Young exhibitors at Haslingden and District Allotments and Horticultural Association's fifteenth annual show, which was held in the Public Hall on September 10, 1932. The Mayoress, Mrs Watson, presents the Haslingden Natural History Society's challenge shield, won by Helmshore Council School, to Evelyn Hall

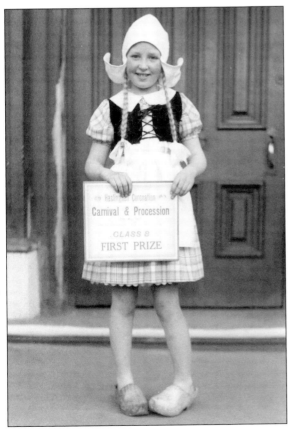

Left: Miss I Emmett, winner of the best juvenile entry in the Corporation's carnival and procession held to mark the coronation of King George VI in 1937

Maypole dancers in Smithies Street, Carrs, in the 1940s. Holding the pole: Susan Entwistle. Holding the ribbons: Irene Barnes, Sheila Hartley, Doreen Bell. Standing: Mary Davison, Doreen Rushton. Smithies Street was demolished in the 1970s

Haslingden Grammar School 1st XI in 1945. Standing: Joe Sherratt (master), K Parker (scorer), J Winter, A Ogden, G Robinson, D Mortimer, R Scott, Bob Whittaker (master). Seated: G Leaf, J Burton, J Ingham, B Ramsbottom, A Morris. Front: J Ward. Seven of these boys, then or later, played in the Lancashire League for either Haslingden or Ramsbottom. John Ingham was professional for several clubs and John Burton made a few appearances for Staffordshire

Above: Haslingden Grammar School Football team in 1948. Back: Arnold Weston (headmaster), F Scot, K Beswick, R Ormerod, Sam Ollerton (groundsman), N Allsop, G Bladen, (?), Bob Whittaker (sports master). Front: T Beswick, H Doherty, J Winter, C Barlow, (?)

Left: Haslingden Youth Club was formed in 1940 to keep young people off the streets during the wartime blackout. It became one of the most successful in the country with more than 250 members during the 1950s.

The club ran many sports teams, organised foreign trips, took part in BBC programmes, staged plays and pantomimes and heard talks by leading figures in public life. Miss Ellen Wilkinson, Minister of Education in the post-war Labour Government, spoke about our efforts to rebuild the devastated cities in Germany and Lord Derby, after describing his family's long association with Lancashire, took part in a game of table tennis.

The adverts shows the wide range of activities during a week in 1945

The club's annual pantomimes attracted large audiences. Here is the cast of *Aladdin*, staged in 1948

Northern Daily Telegraph, Wed., Dec. 13, 1950

A Happy Town?

HASLINGDEN YOUTH CLUB IS ANSWER

MR RHODES BOYSON, a club leader, has compiled a report on Haslingden Youth Club proving that one section of Haslingden's Youth has abundant drive and initiative to make the town a happy home.

Mr Boyson, club leader since his discharge from the Navy, has built up his report in the "mass observation" manner.

Eighty-one boys and 40 girls —total membership of this ten years' old club is 220—completed questionnaires posing a variety of questions.

Facetious answers were the exception rather than the rule. For instance, in reply to the question, "What would you like to do?" six boys wanted to be "spivs," while three chose retirement!

Seventy boys and 34 girls are members of churches and Sunday schools, and 37 boys and 19 girls attend regular night school classes.

Little flirting

Mr Boyson refers to criticisms that the club is "just a flirting place." "In fact," he writes, "flirtation is a very tiny part of club life. Occasionally, one of the older boys will bring along his girl friend, with a shrewd idea, in my opinion, of weighing up how she behaves among people of her own age."

In the questionnaire, the majority of members stated a preference for a mixed club.

The whole man

What is the aim of the club? In Mr Boyson's opinion, "A club's aim should not be to make first-class boxers, footballers or actors, but to help the rounding of the personality, the making of the whole man.

It is perhaps significant that of the employed members, textile workers are in the minority. Is it that "this is a very tiring occupation, causing its workpeople to desire little beyond the passive amusement of the cinema and wireless?" asks Mr Boyson.

Can the club be improved? Suggestions include: More sport, talks, dancing, and an art competition.

Left: Rhodes Boyson, who joined the club as a group leader after leaving the Royal Navy, carried out a survey of members' interests. As this newspaper report shows, he discovered that young people did not place "flirting" high on their list of priorities

The club took part in the 1951 Haslingden Carnival by entering a horse-drawn float that poked fun at local government

Lord Derby, Lord Lieutenant of Lancashire, spoke about his family's role in English history when he visited the club in March, 1955. Afterwards he played table tennis with members and signed authographs. With him are (from the left): Les Witham, Millicent Wood, Trevor Dawson, Audrey Byers, Wendy Laport, Gloria Fox, Kathleen Austin, Lord Derby's assistant, John T Wood (head warden), Lily Whittaker, Keith Hargreaves

The club football team lost to Alder Grange "A" in the play-off for the Rossendale Youth League at Dark Lane in 1956. Back: Raymond Bell, Colin Wallwork, Clifford Moore, Kenneth Allsop, Kevin Wissett, Michael Mernagh, Trevor Dawson, Arnold Warburton. Front: Keith Hargreaves, John Haworth, Graham Lyth, Ron Baron

The cast of *Boy Blue*, the 1956 panto

CUPID AND THE YOUTH CLUB

SCORES of young couples have met at Haslingden Youth Club—and married, the head warden, Mr. John T. Wood, told a youth leaders' conference last weekend.

"It is at the club that we hope they have learned what we are always trying to teach, and which we hope they will try to pass on to their children — Christian Citizenship."

"That should always be the main aim of a youth club, and as far as our own club is concerned I think our record justifies its existence."

Left: The head warden, John T Wood, described the club's activities at a regional conference in 1956. The *Northern Daily Telegraph* highlighted his reference to the fact that cupid was always busy at the club and that many married couples in Haslingden had first met there

Below: Anne Taylor, St Peter's first Patronal Festival Queen, is crowned by Mrs Mary Hardman in 1952

St Peter's Brownies and Guides in the 1950s

Haslingden Modern School Band in 1952. Their teacher and conductor is Joe McQuilton

Classical ballet by Phyllis Flynn and Barbara Hopkinson, both pupils of Miss Beatrice Shipstone in the 1950s

St Mary's morris dancers passing the town centre during the 1958 Rose Queen procession

St Mary's staged pantomimes in the Public hall between 1955 and 1995, invariably playing to full houses. Jack Farrelly and some of the dancers who took part in *Jack and the Beanstalk*, the first production

The full cast of *Jack and the Beanstalk*

Jack Farrelly had another starring role in *Mother Goose* (1962). Joan Atkins was Belinda the Goose, Doreen Howarth the Principal Girl and Maureen Ashe the Principal Boy

Miss Lorna Riley with her class at Haslingden County Primary School in 1958

St Peter's Cubs and Scouts in 1960

The recorder group at Haslingden County Primary School in 1960

The Mayor, Coun. Frank Mitchell, at a cycle rally organised by the town's Accident Prevention Council in May, 1963

More than 350 children went to the Public Hall on March 11, 1969, to hear H E Todd tell them stories. The author of the Bobby Brewster books also lectured on "The Art of Storytelling" to an audience in the County Secondary School. The events were part of National Library Week

Bishop Thomas Holland at the opening of St Mary's County Primary School in Lime Road. The head teacher, Wilf Byrne, is top left

Children from St Peter's in a scene from "Laneside Revue" in 1975

Haslingden High School students take up positions around the prehistoric circle, which was rediscovered on Thirteen Stone Hill in the 1960s by members of Helmshore Local History Society. The site appears to have been used as an astronomical observatory. The extreme setting of the moon, seen from the circle, occurs at Hog Low Pike on the far side of Grane Valley. On Midsummer Day, people walk to the circle to see the sun set over Bleasdale Fell

Beginning in 1984, staff and pupils of Haslingden High School transformed a piece of neglected land between the playing fields and Clod Lane into a thriving nature area. The top picture (with Musbury Tor in the distance) shows the site before work began. *Right:* Eddie Barrett singlehandedly digs a pond, which seven years later (*below*) was praised in a radio broadcast for the wealth of its wildlife

Tree planting on the High School site began at Easter, 1984, when Rossendale Groundwork gave support. This was the first use of the new organisation's logo. The planters are (from the left): Andrew Russell, Paul Kay, Eddie Roberts (teacher), Reece Ward and Paul Kenyon. *Below:* The same spot seven years later: Andrew, Paul, Mr Roberts, Reece and Alan Street are pleased to see how well the trees have grown

Haslingden High School students raised money in 1990 for a "Hazels in Haslingden" scheme. The tree which gave the town its name was in danger of disappearing, but thanks to the youngsters, seen here before a planting session at Lower Cockham, hazels are gaining ground again

RAYS, Rossendale Amateur Operatic Society's youth section, staged *Grease* with great success in 1992

Left: Year 2 pupils of Broadway County Primary School enjoying their "Summer Follies" in 1993

Right: Haslingden Guides organised a Japanese tea party in Townsend Street in 1993 to raise money for the children's ward at Queen's Park Hospital, Blackburn

Left: Haslingden's Millennium celebrations in July, 2000, included activities for children organised by Churches Together in the Sports Centre

Above: St Stephen's Church on its original site in Grane. When the hamlet was largely depopulated following the construction of Ogden reservoir, the church was taken down stone by stone, rebuilt at Three Lane Ends and reconsecrated in 1927. Calf Hey reservoir is on the left of the picture and the Methodist chapel is on the right

Left: Raising the foundation stone from the old site. As the church was taken down, each stone was numbered, as can be seen on the wall in the foreground

Left: The Union Flag flies from the steeple to mark its rebuilding on the new site at Three Lane Ends

Below: The stone heads of Laurence and Nancy Roscow adorn the north facing door at St Stephen's Church, which they did much to promote. Roscow (1826-1873) ran local quarries, and his wife, who lived from 1824 to 1902, was known as "The Queen of Grane". She laid the foundation stone of the church on June 24, 1865

Inside and outside views of the church being taken down

The Bishop of Blackburn, Dr Herbert, arriving at the church for the consecration on May 21, 1927. On the left is the vicar, the Rev A B Harris

St Stephen's illuminated for a visit by the Church Army in 1962

St Stephen's walking day in 1954. The procession is led by the vicar, the Rev Fred Bamber, and the churchwardens, Jack Hartley and Ronald Haworth

Players and officials of Grane Villa in 1957. Standing: Jim Brandwood, Brian Raynor, Harry Hoyle, Norman Grimshaw, John Barnes, Derek Hargreaves, Tom Price, Jack Davies, Jack Parker (President), Peter Hook, Jim Kerron. Seated: Brian Corbridge, Roy Britland, Tom Entwistle, Jack Blundell, Jack Austin, Roland Harker, Barry Maden

The radio and TV star Violet Carson (Ena Sharples of *Coronation Street*) opened the choir fete at St Stephens's on September 22, 1962. With her is the MP for Rossendale, Tony Greenwood (later Lord Greenwood of Rossendale), and the Mayoress, Mrs Annie Mitchell

Helmcroft, Flaxmoss, after the great snow of January, 1940.
Roads and the railway were impassable for several days

Delivering milk in 1907. This photograph, taken on the King's Highway, shows William Grimshaw, of
Coldwells Farm, with his children Jack and Ada

Tree planting at the junction of Blackburn Road and Hudrake in 1907. This was the first of three Arbor Days organised by Haslingden Natural History Society and the short-lived Beautiful Haslingden Council. The other sites were near Alexandra Terrace in Grane Road and opposite "Long Row" at Syke Side. Leading citizens and a child from each school in the borough planted two dozen trees in Blackburn Road. Seven trees have grown to maturity

The military funeral in 1908 of John Walmsley, aged 90, of Ewood Bridge. Mr Walmsley was born at Preston in 1818 and began work in a Manchester cotton mill when he was six. He was a soldier from the age of 20, and took part in all the major battles of the Crimean campaign. When King Edward VII visited Manchester in 1906, Mr Walmsley was one of the veterans chosen to make up the bodyguard. The funeral at Musbury Church attracted hundreds of spectators and crowds also gathered at many points to see the procession make its way from Ewood Bridge, where the photograph was taken

Falling walls wrecked two houses in Parkinson Street and damaged others in Prinny Hill Road when fire swept through Union Foundry on July 16, 1916. About 1,000 tons of cotton waste stored in the building were destroyed

The lower part of what is now Jubilee Road in 1908. Whitaker's Terrace, the row of houses on the far right, was built by the Whitaker family who ran the nearby Grane Road and Holme Spring Mills. Jubilee Road was built in the 1930s and takes its name from the Jubilee in 1935 of King George V

An electric tram approaching the town centre along Blackburn Road in the 1920s. A horse-drawn milk float moves in the opposite direction

A bus negotiates flood water near Worsley Park on April 21, 1931, after a storm caused Hazel Mill reservoir to overflow into Blackburn Road

Haslingden Corporation marked King George V's Silver Jubilee in 1935 by illuminating a bus. With it are Fred Duckworth (Chief Assistant, Electricity and Transport Department), W T Hilder (Borough Electrical Engineer and Transport Manager) and Harold Kay (Transport Depot manager). After the celebrations, the "Haslingden's Tribute" sign was fixed to the Corporation's portable toilet, where it remained for many years

Above: The start of celebrations to mark the Coronation of King George VI began on May 12, 1937 (Coronation Day), when the bellringers at the Parish Church signalled the start of festivities with an 8am peal. Musbury bells also rang

Left: Coronation Day ended with the lighting of bonfires on Hutch Bank and Musbury Tor. A torchlight procession left the municipal offices at 9.20pm and made its way to Hutch Bank (pictured). At 10 o'clock a rocket sent up from the town centre gave the signal to light the fires

Above: On Saturday, May 15, the last day of the celebrations, local businesses, churches and other organisations took part in a carnival and procession. Here floats are gathering in Marsden Square. The route was King Street, Hudrake, Blackburn Road, Brook Street, Hud Hey Road, Blackburn Road, Lower Deardengate, Helmshore Road, St Peter's Avenue, Manchester Road, Deardengate, George Street, Marsden Square. An unbroken line of spectators, four to six deep, stretched from Hud Hey to the town centre

Left: Haslingden Co-operative Society entered a float in the procession. The picture was taken at the top of Deardengate

"The Birth of Methodism" was the theme of the float from Manchester Road Methodist Sunday School. These members depicted the Holy Club

Haslingden Amateur Swimming Club put on a gala that lasted for more than three hours. The event aroused enormous interest, and there was a queue of ticket holders outside the Public Baths an hour and a half before the door opened

Mills, as well as providing work for most Haslingden and Helmshore people, also contributed to the social and sporting life of the district. Here is the cast of a revue given in 1944 by workpeople of Hazel Mill and their children

The Arts Club Choir in 1950

Left: Geoffrey Jackson, David Flynn and Colin Darwen in a sketch from *Flight of Fancy*, Haslingden Arts Club's 1961 revue

Below: Rossendale Amateur Operatic Society scored one of its many triumphs when it gave *My Fair Lady* in Haslingden Public Hall in 1969. Here is the full cast

A scene from Haslingden Arts Club's 1970 production of *Oh What a Lovely War!* Front (from the left): Geoffrey Jackson, Mary Haworth, Shirley Dawson, Peter Ibbs and Stanley Whittaker

When the town council decided that the Big Lamp in the Market Place had become a danger to traffic, they had no plans to resite it. This well-loved piece of Haslingden's heritage would have gone for scrap had not Donald Heyworth found a new home for it in his garden at Rothdene, Helmshore Road. Here Haslingden bandsmen mark the restoration of gas lighting in December, 1963

Victoria Park in 1972 before the Haslingden by-pass changed the look of Flaxmoss. Manchester Road can be seen at the top of the picture and Helmshore Road in the foreground

Sykeside House in the 1970s, when the road to Rawtenstall ran beside the garden wall. James Stott, woollen manufacturer at Sykeside Mill and a prominent Methodist, built the house c.1840. A blue plaque donated by the Rawsthorne Society, records that the composer Alan Rawsthorne lived here from 1908 to 1913. In the 1960s, Sykeside House was the home of the actor William Roche (Ken Barlow in *Coronation Street*). It is now a country hotel

On the cold and blustery afternoon of March 18, 1974, the Mayor of Haslingden, Alderman Donald Butterworth, cuts the first sod to initiate work on the £250,000 Sports Centre at Flaxmoss. Haslingden Recreational Development Organisation, chaired by Jack Whittaker, raised £40,000 for the scheme. Sir Robin Brook, National Sports Council chairman, officially opened the centre on September 6, 1975

Hen pens were a familiar sight in Haslingden and Helmshore during the first half of the last century. Members of the Rodwell family ran large poultry farms at Kenyon Clough and Deansgate, part of which is shown here. The Haslingden by-pass crosses this land. Flash Mill (now demolished) can be seen behind the houses in Jubilee Road

George McKenzie, captain of Grane Villa FC, holds the challenge trophy after his side won the final of the 1961 Cup and Medals competition on St Mary's playing field. Villa beat the Callopies, a family team from Rawtenstall, 3-1 in a muddy encounter

A busy day at the Trustee Savings Bank, Deardengate, in the 1960s

The 15th Rossendale Girl Guides celebrated their silver jubilee in 1962 with a party at the Grammar School. The Mayoress, Mrs Annie Mitchell, cuts the cake watched by (from the left) Mrs Eatough (Divisional Commissioner); Mrs Fenwick (District Commissioner); Miss Lorna Riley; Mr Arnold Weston (headmaster HGS); the Mayor, Coun Frank Mitchell; Mrs A Kirby and Mrs J Fuller

Girls representing local firms taking part in a competition organised by the *Rossendale Free Press*. Jack Taylor, the newspaper's advertising representative, is on the right

The Hollies at the junction of Rising Bridge and Hud Hey Roads in 1967. David Halstead, industrialist, MP for Rossendale and local historian, lived in the house in the early years of the 20th century. It was the Stonefold vicarage from 1907 to 1956 and is now a nursing home

Holland's food factory at Rising Bridge has long been an institution in the pie-loving north of England. The company sells $1\frac{1}{2}$m pies each week, with leading sports clubs in all parts of the country among the growing list of customers. Here is the workforce in 1987, with the managing director, Mr Graham March, in the centre of the front row

Two flowering cherry trees in the Memorial Gardens commemorate the first sixty years of the Girl Guide movement. The Mayoress, Mrs Joyce Valentine, contributed to the local celebrations in November, 1970, by planting the first tree. She is watched by Mrs Annie Cliffe, Haslingden's longest serving Guider, who planted the second

Haslingden Choir in 1977

Rossendale Amateurs chose *The Merry Widow* for their 1984 production. From the left: Sandra Walsh, Maureen Jackson, Brenda Wilkinson and Yvonne Russell

The first balloon flight from Haslingden provided much excitement for the two passengers. Bill Grimshaw (*left*) and Graham Woodcock. The hot air balloon took off from Haslingden cricket field on September 7, 1986, and landed in Rochdale, where it narrowly avoided a train. The report appeared in the *Rochdale Observer*

Train-halt alert for airborne attraction

A MANCHESTER-bound train made an unscheduled stop near Rochdale Hornets ground on Saturday night . . . for a hot-air balloon.

The balloon floated clear before making a bumpy landing in a school playing field near the Hornets ground.

It had taken off with its three-man crew 35 minutes earlier from Haslingden Cricket Club ground.

After cruising the moors it skimmed roof-tops on the outskirts of Rochdale and hovered over the Town Hall attracting hundreds of sightseers.

Haslingden remembered the Irish patriot Michael Davitt (1846-1906) on the 50th anniversary of his death and 150th anniversary of his birth. Davitt spent his youth in the town, where, in the Mechanics' Institution (now the Public Library) he first read the history of his native land. The top picture shows some of the people who attended the unveiling, on May 12, 1956, of the memorial on the site of the Davitt family home in Wilkinson Street. John Bourke (seated) suggested the memorial, which was unveiled by Mr W J Loughrey (on Mr Bourke's right), a Liverpool barrister, who knew Davitt. On Mr Bourke's left is Davitt's son, Dr Robert Davitt. Among others in the picture are the Mayor and Mayoress, Coun and Mrs J W Everett; the Irish Ambassador, Mr Frederick H Boland; and Mr Anthony Greenwood, the local MP.

Left: Jim Higgins TD, the Irish Government's Chief Whip and Minister of State, unveiling a blue plaque at the library. The ceremony on 24 March, 1996, was among a number of events arranged by the Irish community and local historians to mark the anniversary of Davitt's birth. Lancashire County Council provided the plaque. Mr Higgins is pictured with the Mayor of Rossendale, Coun Alan Fishwick, and Davitt's grandson, Father Thomas Davitt

Three Haslingden chess players, John Ward, John Haworth and Arnold Chadwick, pit their skills against the Lancashire champion, Mr C G Hilton in Haslingden Conservative Club

Left: Helmshore's memorial to the 53 men killed in World War I is a park, a playing field and a 40ft clock tower on land given by Mr Oliver Porritt. The clock tower cost £2,320 and the bells £560. The people of Helmshore, Ewood Bridge and Irwell Vale contributed almost £1,000 and Mr Porritt provided the rest. The official opening took place in June, 1922

Above: Helmshore on April 16, 1904, the day the Liberal Club bowling green opened. The banner on the side of the club says "Success and long life to the donors"

Musbury Tor taken from Top o' th' Brow in the early 1900s. Part of Higher Mill can be seen bottom left and the photograph also shows Middle Hollin Bank Farm, also on the left

These photographs of Burnt Hill Farm were taken in the 1960s, when many abandoned buildings in Musbury were fast falling into ruin. The 18th century farm was known as a laithe house because the living quarters, barn and shippon were all under one roof. The lower picture shows the curving boundary of Musbury deer park, which was enclosed in 1305

The pilot died when his Cessna aircraft crashed into Musden Head Moor during a night navigation flight on June 1, 1981. Brian Wilkinson, of Nantwich, had taken off from Speke Airport, near Liverpool

Left: Higher Tanpits Farm in Musbury Valley. The photograph dates from 1984, two years before the building was demolished. Eighteenth century deeds mention tanpits on the site

Below: Bathing belles in Musbury Brook in 1930. The girl in the tree is Mary Nuttall

Carr Lane Cottages in 1960. Carr is an old local word for Alder tree. A stone over the barn door had the inscription "Thomas & Mary Worswick, 1823". The family ran the nearby Slidings cotton mill

Known as "The Mansion" or "The Castle", this mid 17th century building at Tor End Lane Farm occupies one of the oldest settlement sites in the district

Above: A view of Tor from the tenter field adjoining Gregory Fold Lane and the railway. When the photograph was taken in the early 1900s, woollen cloth from Higher Mill was still being taken to the fields to dry, having first been stretched on tenter hooks fixed to the frames. Some of these were very old. One was called "Napoleon"; another "The Great Eastern" after Brunel's great steamship. Park Mill in the middle distance was built by John Tattersall in 1864, extended by Worsley and Haworth in 1893 and by J H Birtwistle & Co in 1914

Helmshore Local History Society revived the Musbury Tor Mile in 1958, and hundreds of young men have since raced to the top of the hill and back. The top picture shows the juniors setting off from Barlow Terrace in 1961; and *right*, a special cheer for Alan Schofield, "last man" in 1963

Above: Sunnybank Cottages (built 1882 onwards) and Torside House in the early 1900s. The field in the foreground is now a wood

Left: Alden Valley looking towards Musbury Tor. This early 20th century photograph shows the lane that ran from Clough cottages to the river and also the newly-built Tor Side Lodge

Holcombe Hunt at the junction of Holcombe Road and Free Lane in the 1930s

Sunnybank Mill, famous for its papermakers' felts — Bank of England notes depended on them — seen from the Alden Valley in 1900. Private houses now occupy the site. In front of Sunnybank Cottages is a crane for handling stone from Alden Quarry. Many of the "Porritt" houses on the seafront at St Anne's were shaped here. W J Porritt, who ran the mill, did more than anyone to ensure the growth of the resort

The Rolls-Royce used during the 1920s by Roland Spencer, a director of Porritts & Spencers, Woollen manufacturers. The company's Sunnybank Mill is in the background

Left: "4 balls for 6d". Mrs Sheila Greenhow takes aim during a Guides' garden party at Moorfields in 1952

Right: Haymaking at Heatherlands, Helmshore, in the early 1940s. The field beyond the fence is now Alden Rise, and houses also cover the hayfield. Charles Simpson stands on the cart, and Charles, Jnr holds the rake

Left: The wash tower overlooking the Sunnybank Mill of Porritts & Spencers in 1960. It was used at an earlier time when woollen cloth was taken out of doors to dry on tenter frames. During World War II, the building was a post for Air Raid Wardens. It was demolished in 1988

Heatherlands Garage in Holcombe Road, Helmshore; a photograph taken during a get-together of Bentley owners in 1950

Anne and Richard Pilling in their general store at 482 Holcombe Road in the 1960s. The customer is Clarence Entwistle, who conducted the village brass band for many years

Hollinbank c.1900. The Mechanics Arms was built in 1881 by Thomas Mercer, of Spring Bank Brewery, Edenfield, to replace an earlier pub. In 1927, the building became the British Legion Club, which survived until 1996. It is now a private house. The largely 19th century cottages next to the pub were demolished in 1974. On the other side of Holcombe Road is the old Bar House, where tolls were taken in the early days of the Bury-Blackburn turnpike. The open space in the foreground was previously occupied by a row of back-to-back houses, nicknamed "Cockroach Row"

Children and their gifts at a Musbury Sunday School bazaar in the late 1920s

Helmshore Old Folk's Treat on 9 April, 1932. The photograph, taken in the Primitive Methodist Sunday School, shows the Mayoress, Mrs Watson, with the oldest lady and gentleman: Mrs Rhodes, of Holden Wood, aged 85, and Mr William Fitton, of Wood Bank, who was 82. There were 182 guests aged 65 and over. The men received cigarettes and tobacco; the women chocolates. This was the year in which the treat was revived. As early as 1872, the former township of Musbury began yearly treats, but they ceased on the outbreak of World War I

Before the developers came. The village seen from Tanner Bank in the early 1900s

The annual "Mothers' Tea" at Springhill Sunday School in December, 1954

"The Building of the Church" by the Junior Guild provided the centrepiece of the Harvest Festival at Springhill Methodist Church in 1955

Above: Primary scholars of Springhill Methodist Sunday School who took part in the Christmas Show in 1959. *Below right:* A hat parade arranged by Helmshore Methodists raised money for medical missions in 1966. Garth Dawson's picture shows Mrs Annie Mitchell and Lynne Ashton

Above: Heather Simpson, Helmshore Methodist Church's Harvest Queen, and her attendants in 1974

Christmas celebrations at Springhill Methodist Sunday School in the late 1950s. The Minister is the Rev George Kenny

Smiling in the rain. Barbara Mudd, Margaret Ramsbottom, Gwen Fitton, Christine Mitchell and Jean Hamer braved the weather to take part in the 1955 United Methodist Whit Procession

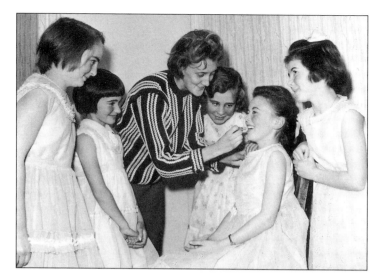

Members of Helmshore Methodist Youth Club preparing for their Gang Show in 1963. Valerie Barlow puts the final touches to 11-year-old Lynne Ashton's make-up, watched by Rebecca West, Glenys Readshaw, Sheila Waller and Carole Ashton

Lynne Ashton was Helmshore Methodist's Harvest Queen in 1967. With her (from the left) are Andrew Pearson, Mrs Pat Haynes, Janet Mills, Denise Stott, Heather Simpson, Caroline Woods and Ruth Barnes

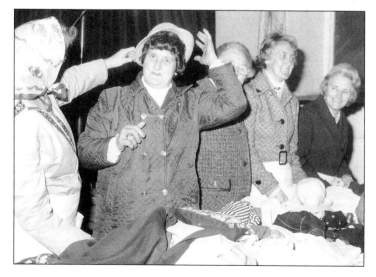

A jumble sale at Helmshore Methodist Church in 1978. Left to right: Pat Fisher, Louise Hamnett, Nellie Hall, Valerie Riding and Marion Readshaw

Left: Workmen laying a water main in Bowl Alley in 1906. Middle Mill, now My Travel (Airtours), is on the left

Above: Joe Crook, cycle maker, ironmonger and lamplighter, with his wife and daughter Alice, outside their shop in Tanpits (Spring Gardens) in 1910. The shop was the third in the row from the Gregory Fold end

Above: The weaving shed at Middle Mill before World War I. Weavers ran four or six looms each; and because of the noise, they communicated by lip reading. The girl in the foregound is May Hannah Walsh. Behind her is Maggie Schofield

During the 1930s and again after World War II, football teams from mills, workshops and other organisations competed in highly popular "cup and medals" knock-out games. In 1930, when Haslingden Church Institute promoted the competition, Park Mill, Helmshore (top picture) drew with Carr Parkers in both the final and the replay. Only medals were presented, but in the following year, Park Mill beat Springvale 3-1 in another replayed final before 5,000 spectators at Prinny Hill. The lower picture shows the team officials and supporters on the Holme Field. Tommy Rogers captained the side in both seasons. Park Mill's triumph inspired Mrs E Bacon to compose a poem

Haslingden C. of E. Medal Competition.

Well done you Park Mill players!
You have won the football game;
Thirty-two teams competed,
And yours is the honoured name.

You have won the Silver Rose Bowl,
You have won the gold medals too;
You kept your pluck to the finish,
Helmshore should be proud of you.

There were crowds of men and women,
All dressed in various hues;
There were shouts of "Come on Yellows"
And "Boot it, you White and Blues"

'Twas very hard luck that evening,
When each team tried more and more;
And the "Ref" blew the final whistle,
And it ended without a score.

Many were disappointed,
Many went home with a sigh;
Some were almost fainting
And others felt ready to die.

But the final date was mentioned,
And fixed for the first of May,
And the competition came to a close
In a very friendly way.

Alderman Sutcliffe presented the Trophy,
As each player stood side by side,
And they all received their medals,
With a certain amount of pride.

And "Park Mill" Lads were the winners
With three good goals to one
And "Spring Vale" took it bravely,
And were ready to say "Well Done."

By Mrs E. Bacon of Helmshore.

When milk was delivered by horse-drawn floats. Maggie Barnes
and Harry Berry at Park House Farm in 1930

In November, 1971, a Wessex 60 Helicopter helped to lay a natural gas pipeline across the lower
parts of Alden and Musbury for the North Western Gas Board. Higher Mill chimney is on the right

In 2001, Transco awarded a much larger contract to the Australian company, McConnell Dowell, for a pipeline linking Helmshore and Samlesbury. The route was behind Tor. These pictures show work in progress at the head of the Musbury Valley and in Alden

St Thomas's held a pageant in 1914 to raise money for reseating the church. The procession went from the National School to Haslingden and returned via Grane Road and Holcombe Road to the Holme field. Here the floats are passing Weirfoot. The rose queen was Mary Edith Tattersall, of Westbourne

A 1920s photograph of a solid-tyred lorry delivering hay to Helmshore. The men are (from the left) Harry Haworth, Jack Metcalfe and Harry Metcalfe. The Bridge End Hotel is on the right

The Memorial Gardens and its clock tower were given to the village by the Porritt family in 1921. A plaque records the names of the men who died during the two world wars and a service is held close by on each Armistice Sunday. The upper photograph was taken on Armistice Day, 1922. Behind the tower is the now-vanished amphitheatre, where brass bands gave concerts and on one occasion (below), where Miss May Warburton recited poetry. A choir of singers from local churches also took part in the entertainment

Led by the Mayor of Haslingden, Councillor Ben Fisher, the Musbury Church Walking Day procession heads down Free Lane on May 25, 1958. Other adults in the picture are (from the left): Harry Broadbent, Joyce Cockerill, Freda Grimshaw, Joyce Bargh, Tom Worswick (Mayor's Attendant) and Jim Bonner (Vicar's Warden)

The three Helmshore churches held a joint procession through the village in June, 1955. The picture shows hymn singing at the foot of Free Lane

Mary Horrocks, the new Rose Queen, leads the Springhill procession along Bowl Alley in July, 1933. A "Village Wedding" group can be seen in the background

New Barn Farm in 1953. Beyond the building was a footpath to Higher Cockham and Rossendale Golf Course. New Barn Close commemorates the vanished farmhouse

Bowl Alley (Station Road) and Elm Terrace with a drapery shop on the corner. The stone pillars, which now stand at the entrance to the lane to Snighole, came from Horncliffe House, Townsendfold, in 1920, soon after this picture was taken. The iron fence has been replaced by a hedge

Snighole in 1905. Snig is an old word for eel, a fish once common in the River Ogden. The three-storey building on the left was once the home of handloom weavers

Above: Snighole Cottages in October, 1960, when the dwellings were still back-to-back

Left: Ravenshore with its rock pools, so convenient for bathing, was once known as "Little Blackpool". This photograph was taken on a hot day in 1904

Above left: Jeanette Bonner operating a spinning jenny built in 1964 for Helmshore Local History Society. Derek Pilkington made the frame in the attic of his home in Elm Terrace and because it was too big to negotiate the stairs, it was lowered to the ground from the attic window. TMM (Research), who were then experimenting with the latest spinning technology, agreed to provide the metal parts for the machine patented by James Hargreaves, of Oswaldtwistle, in 1770

Above right: Textile mills took on a striking new character when lit up at night. This is the Bridge End Mill of Porritts and Spencers in 1961. The firm used the top floor for wool sorting and the rest for storage. Fire destroyed the mill on January 15, 1982

George Bentley sorting wool at Bridge End Mill in the 1950s

Above left: A tense moment on the bowling green of Sunnybank Social Club. Jack Pilling (chairman) and David Penman are on the right. *Above right:* Watched by his captain Peter Brown, Tom Watson prepares to bowl for Sunnybank

Left: Sunnybank won the Bray Cup when they became champions of the Haslingden Bowling League in 1991. Pictured on the Haslingden Conservative Club green are (from the left): Andrew Billington, Walter Gregson, Jim O'Connor, Robert Haworth, Jack Buckley (capt), Malcolm Padley, Fred Barlow, Tom Watson and Michael Jefferson

A train arriving at Helmshore railway station in the early 1900s. The line between Stubbins and Accrington opened in 1848 and closed in 1966

The strong men. The brothers William and Charles Hollin were champion weightlifters, who, in the early years of the 19th century, ran the Hollin School of Physical Culture in an old building on a site now occupied by Lodge Bank. They also gave exhibitions throughout east Lancashire

Albert Drinkwater, who was postman in Helmshore, toured the music halls in the early 1900s using the stage name Silva Rita. He mastered several musical instruments and played the violin behind his back. Albert, who appeared with Charlie Chaplin, Houdini, Vesta Tilley and other stars, died in 1953

Pub grub. Staff from TMM (Research), Helmshore, enjoying pie and peas at the Station Hotel in 1958. In the centre is Jack Blundell, who played cricket for Haslingden

More than 200 Scouts, Cubs, Guides and brownies marched from St Thomas's Church to the Sunday School in Holcombe Road in March, 1952, following the dedication of the Scouts' new colours

Above: Piccadilly, built in the 1820s for workpeople employed by W & R Turner, woollen manufacturers, pictured in the spring of 1960, a year before its demolition. The two upper floors were back-to-back with St Thomas Street

Left: Helmshore Road in the 1950s. The post office is on the right. The wooden building on the left was a doctor's surgery, and that next to the houses a fish and chip shop first run by Sidney Nuttall. Piccadilly is behind the old Co-op store

Above: Joe Haworth with Red Rose, his pigeon, that outflew hundreds of birds from east Lancashire to win the Nantes Race in 1960. Red Rose was released from Nantes at 6am and reached Helmshore at 4.30pm. With Joe outside his loft near Higher Mill are sons Brian and Bobby

Left: In March, 1974, the steeple of Musbury Church received new clock faces made from Perspex. The vicar, Rev Stuart Winward, climbed the scaffolding to help with the work

A ceremony at St Thomas's Church in January, 1975, marked the completion by Miss Ethel Bentley of 70 years as a Sunday School teacher. She took her first class when she was 15. The vicar, Rev Stuart Winward, presented Miss Bentley with an address watched by (from the left) Tom Mead (Sunday School superintendent), George Heckinbottom, (churchwarden), Tom Watson (teacher), Mrs Margaret Astbury (teacher) and Ken Rothwell (churchwarden)

July, 1976, saw the start of work on St Thomas's new Sunday School. The ceremony of cutting the first turf was performed by Miss Ethel Bentley, the oldest teacher, and Tom Mead, superindendent

Lynne Johnstone (Cinderella) and Carole Vizzard (Buttons), two of the stars of Musbury Players' 1995 pantomime.

A scene from the 2001 panto, *Beauty and the Beast*, which the group staged to mark its tenth anniversary

St Thomas's Local History Group, formed in 1998, holds regular meetings and lectures, visits places of interest and stages exhibitions

St Thomas's has encouraged youth activities for many years and Girl Guides have been active since 1932. Here is a 2002 group with (back row) Wendy Heap (Unit helper) and Jayne Brierley (Guider) and (Left, middle row) Mhairi Brady (Assistant Guider)

Left: The Cubs with (From the left) Pauline Lomas (Kaa), Gillian Cooper (Akela) and Victoria March (Baloo)

Right: The Musbury Rainbows with (from the left) Helena Wensley (Rainbow Guider), Kiera Maden (Young Leader), Aimee Brierley (Young Leader) and Kate Hill (Unit Helper)

Below: The Brownies with (from the left) Sue Greenwood (helper), Audrey Mitchell (Brown Owl), Carol Wensley (Divisional Commissioner) and Glenis Gardner (Brown Owl)

Members of Helmshore Co-operative Society in a field at the end of East Street in July, 1906. Only Nos 2 to 14 had then been built

Miss Pollard with her class at Helmshore Primary School in 1950

The head teacher at Helmshore County Primary School, John Jenkinson, supervises a game of rounders on the school field in the late 1950s

Methodists FC in 1966. Back: Kenneth Riding, Robert Haworth, Alan Isherwood, Frank Ashworth, Ronnie Wolfenden, Fred Barlow. Front: David Haworth, John Wadsworth, Keith Riding, Colin Mitchell, Jack Pilling

Right: The first children to attend St Veronica's RC Primary School which opened in 1974

Below: The Bishop of Salford, the Rev Thomas Holland, with children and staff of St Veronica's in 1975. On the left is the Bishop's secretary, Mons. John Allen and on the right the parish priest, Father James Christie. The head teacher is Mrs Annette Allen

Left: A skipping race at St Veronica's in 1977

Members of St Thomas's made schooldays the theme of their carnival in 1987. The vicar, the Rev Alan Sowerbutts, is third from the left

Broadway seen from Gregory Fold in the early 1950s. The much loved tree in its circular stone base was later removed when the road was widened

Haslingden Borough Band at Flaxmoss House, the home of their president, William Landless, in 1953. The conductor is Joe McQuilton. The band had gained the *Daily Herald Challenge Tribute* (the Eagle Star Trophy), seen in the foreground, for winning the North West area qualifying contest (Section 4)

The River Ogden in flood following the storm on June 17, 2002. The waterfall near the junction of Station Road and Holcombe Road is barely visible.

Jim and Julie Walsh picking cherries from one of the 2,600 trees they have planted on three acres of hillside facing their home in Holcombe Road. They began to create their orchard and wood in 1994 and when this book went to press in 2002, some forty kinds of tree were flourishing. Helmshore Local History Society donated fifty trees in 2001 to mark its first half century

Helmshore County Primary School celebrated the Queen's Golden Jubilee in June, 2002 with a patriotic party. Enjoying themselves here are (from the left): Daniel Mousley, Thomas Phillips, Joseph Williams and Rory Potts